FLUSH!

The Scoop on Poop

Throughout the Ages

BY CHARISE MERICLE HARPER

 LITTLE, BROWN AND COMPANY

New York ❧ Boston ❧ London

ALSO BY CHARISE MERICLE HARPER:

Imaginative Inventions

There Was a Bold Lady Who Wanted a Star

FOR IVY AND OWEN,
WHO THINK POOPY JOKES ARE SOOOO FUNNY!
...AND CONRAD TOO.

Little, Brown and Company

Time Warner Book Group
1271 Avenue of the Americas, New York, NY 10020
Visit our Web site at www.lb-kids.com

First Edition: March 2007

Library of Congress Cataloging-in-Publication Data

Harper, Charise Mericle.
    Flush! : the scoop on poop throughout the ages / by Charise Mericle Harper. — 1st ed.
       p. cm.
    ISBN 0-316-01064-2 (hardcover)
    1. Toilets—History—Juvenile literature. 2. Toilets—Social aspects—Juvenile literature. I. Title.
GT476.H35 2006
392.3'6—dc22   2005015080

10 9 8 7 6 5 4 3 2 1

TWP

Printed in Singapore

The illustrations for this book were done in acrylic and collage on chipboard.
The text was set in Abadi MT, and the display type is Keener.

TABLE OF CONTENTS

Romans bleached their tunics
in urine to make them clean.
Eskimos washed their hair
with urine to give it sheen.

But that's not all that urine has done.
It's really been used by everyone.

American Indians and Eskimos
used urine to tan hides.
The Spanish cleaned their teeth with it,
and then they smiled wide.

The French added it to fertilizer
so that their plants would grow.
Columbians put it in their food
to salt up stews and dough.

It's been used in dyes
and to clean out eyes,
so it's no surprise
that some think it's wise
to drink a cup
as a pick-me-up.

They swear by it and say,
"We do it every day!
And when we're feeling sick,
it always does the trick."

Urine has been used by cultures all over the world to cure health ailments, and for ceremonial reasons, too. Human urine is composed of 95 percent water, 2.5 percent urea, and 2.5 percent calcium, phosphates, sodium, and ammonium. Ammonium breaks down into ammonia, which is an excellent cleaning agent!

BEFORE TOILET PAPER

Empty coconut shells,
grass, straw, and hay.
For some a wet left hand
to wipe the muck away.

Fancy lace, hemp,
a catalog from Sears,
cold snow, or tundra moss
for clean and shiny rears.

Pages from a book,
newsprint, corncobs, sand,
mussel shells, and wool,
a rock held in a hand.

A sponge on a stick,
a scraper made of wood.
And so they cleaned their bottoms
as best as they could.

THE LEFT HAND   REALIZATION   CALL TO ACTION   CONCENTRATION   SATISFACTION

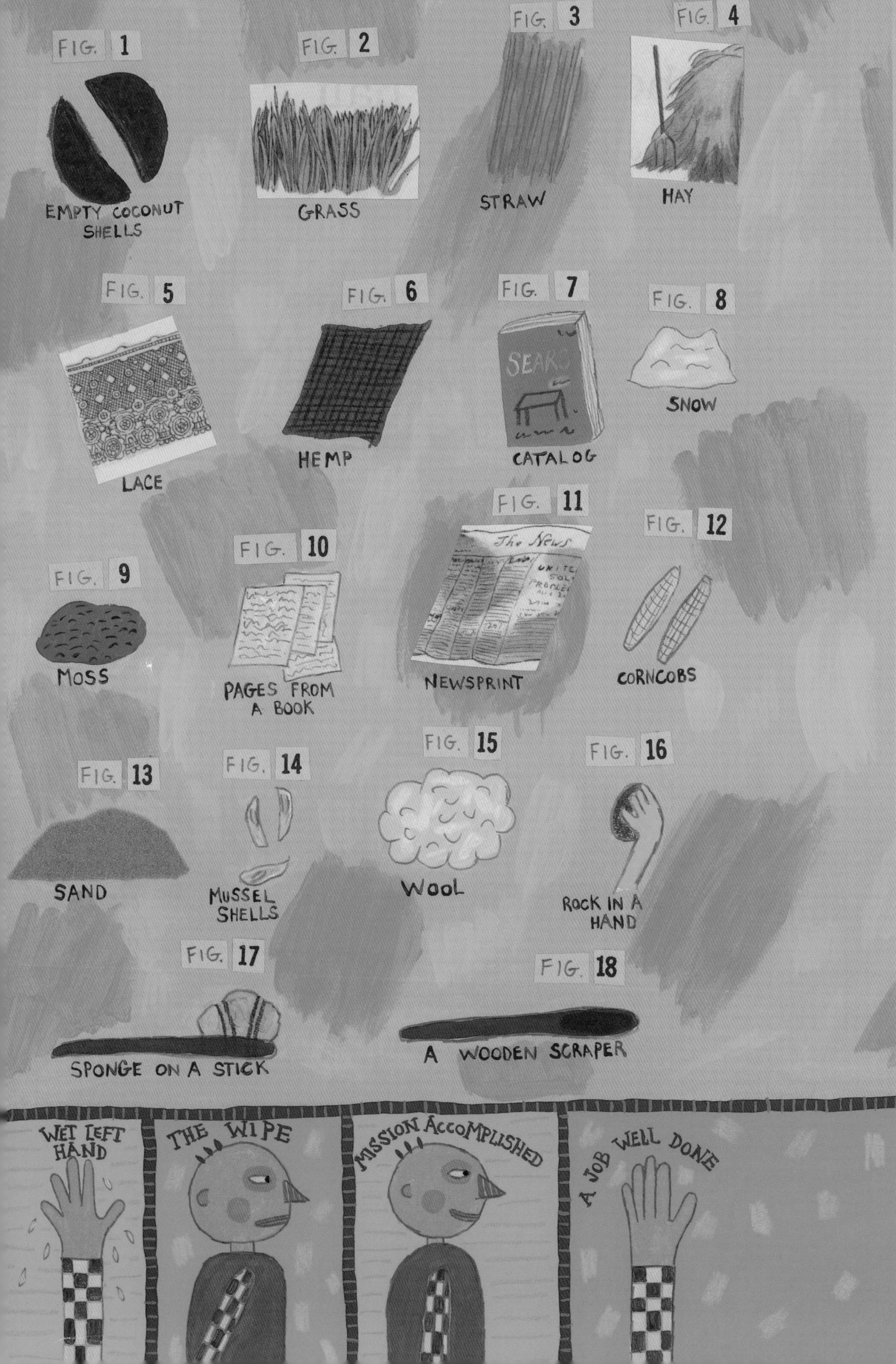

FIG. 1
EMPTY COCONUT
SHELLS

FIG. 2
GRASS

FIG. 3
STRAW

FIG. 4
HAY

FIG. 5
LACE

FIG. 6
HEMP

FIG. 7
SEAR
CATALOG

FIG. 8
SNOW

FIG. 9
MOSS

FIG. 10
PAGES FROM
A BOOK

FIG. 11
The News
UNITE
SOL:
PROPLE
AU 5
NEWSPRINT

FIG. 12
CORNCOBS

FIG. 13
SAND

FIG. 14
MUSSEL
SHELLS

FIG. 15
WOOL

FIG. 16
ROCK IN A
HAND

FIG. 17
SPONGE ON A STICK

FIG. 18
A WOODEN SCRAPER

WET LEFT
HAND

THE WIPE

MISSION ACCOMPLISHED

A JOB WELL DONE

LOOK WHAT I FOUND.

OOHH!

E X C A V A T I O N

Toilets were invented
over 10,000 years ago,
and it's by digging in the dirt
that we know what we know.

Scotland is the place,
archaeologists say,
where they've found the first pipes
that carried human waste away.

In the areas known as Pakistan
and Syria today,
ancient people also used
pipes and water in this way.

Nothing was too special
for the Minoans of Crete.
Rainwater flushed their toilets,
quite a sanitation feat.

And there was something else
(something others couldn't beat)—
they fit all their toilets
with a comfy wooden seat.

The Cloaca Maxima
is a tunnel under Rome
that was built to carry sewage
away from the Roman home.

Built around 500 BC
and sixteen feet wide—
that's 43 sandwiches long
if you lay them side by side.

Not every house could use it.
There was a price to pay,
so many of the poor
couldn't flush their waste away.

Rome had public toilets
where men would sit and chat.
And while doing their business
they could talk of this and that.

Waste floated by in trenches
and everyone could see
what others had done
in the open publicly.

Bottoms were cleaned
with a sponge on a stick.
Kept in a pail of water,
it seemed to do the trick.

Did they change the water?
No! Not frequently.
So bottom one was cleaner
than bottom twenty-three.

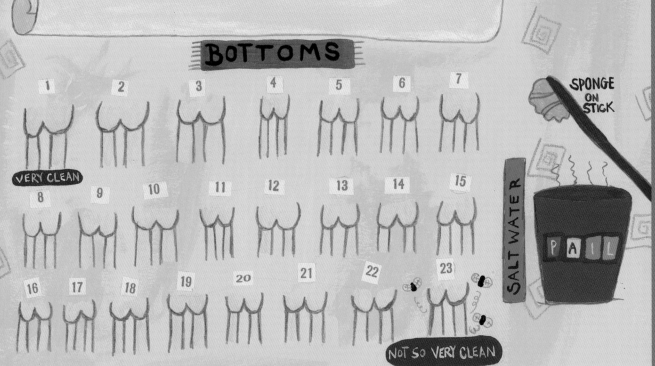

BOTTOMS

1 2 3 4 5 6 7

VERY CLEAN

8 9 10 11 12 13 14 15

16 17 18 19 20 21 22 23

NOT SO VERY CLEAN

SALT WATER

PAIL

SPONGE ON STICK

FUN FACTS

Parts of the Cloaca Maxima are still used today. The public toilets were set up with rows of seats out in the open. In front of the seats was a trough, and the sewage from the patrons farther up floated by on its way out. Each seat was equipped with a sponge on a stick soaking in a bucket of saltwater.

BAD SANITATION DAYS

WAIT
FOR
ME!

In medieval times
conditions were not clean.
Filth was a part of life
for the peasant, king, and queen.

More people lived in cities
than had lived in them before,
so cleaning sewage waste
was something of a chore.

People threw it out of windows
or they threw it in a pit.
They dropped it in the road
and sometimes even buried it.

The streets were open sewers
with filth just floating by,
sometimes even blocking roads
when the mounds of it were high.

They dumped it outside city gates,
where the piles just grew and grew.
And no one seemed to know
what it was that they should do.

The smell was unbelievable—
rank beyond compare—
only pleasing to the flies
that were buzzing in the air.

Farmers said they'd take some:
"It'll fertilize my crop."
But the piles kept getting bigger
'cause it's something you can't stop.

Think about your toilet needs
for just a single day,
and then multiply the bottoms—
that's a lot to throw away.

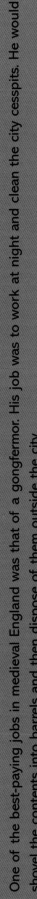

There is a place on a castle wall,
a little room, not much at all.
You sit down on a hard stone seat
and wait to pass the food you eat.

And what you've eaten
falls in the moat,
where it might sink
or it might float.

It's stinky.
It's smelly.
It's brown.
It's thick.
This moat of sludge could make you sick.

An attacking knave
would have to be brave
to cross this muck
and not get stuck.

And if he was
a really good shot,
he'd try to catch you
on the pot.

He'd shoot an arrow,
pierce your rear,
hear you yelp,
and then give a cheer.

ARROW

FUN FACTS

The word *garderobe* means "wardrobe." The castle moat was used as a place to dispose of all waste material from the castle. There were two types of garderobes—those built on the outside of a castle wall and those built in the interior of the castle. During an attack against the castle, the enemy could climb the castle wall and get into the castle through the hole in the garderobe. Not a grand entrance, but still effective.

THE HOW-TOS OF THE CHAMBER POT
(FRANCE 1300-EARLY 1600s)

What, you ask, is a chamber pot?
Well, here are things that it is not.
It's not a pot to keep your money,
pretty flowers, toys, or honey.

 **MONEY**   **TREATS**   **TOYS**   **HONEY**   **COZY IN BED**

HEAD

Don't put that pot upon your head.
Don't cozy up with it in bed.
Don't look inside it for a treat.
Don't use that pot to wash your feet.

PLAIN

 **foot WASHING**

But if at night you have to go
(and feel some rumblings down below)
and toilets aren't invented yet,
a chamber pot is your best bet.

ABOVE   **BELOW**

FANCY

But now it's full, what do you do?
Don't keep it in the house with you.

Lean out your window, give a shout
because it's time to throw it out.
You yell a warning: "Gardez l'eau!"
(GAR-day low),
then empty it on the street below.

And those below look up and say,
"Run, quick! We have to get away.
Move your feet and don't get stuck
or you'll be covered in stinky muck!"

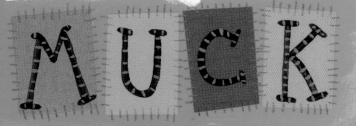

FUN FACTS

Disposing of chamber pots into the street was a practice retained from Roman times. The English used the word "gardyloo" as a warning and often still refer to the toilet as the "loo." Supposedly, men with good manners walked on the left-hand side of women to shield them from falling filth.

THE FIRST (MECHANICAL) FLUSHING TOILET

Characters: Queen Elizabeth I and Sir John Harrington

In 1596
the godson of the queen
made the first mechanical toilet
the court had ever seen.

He named his toilet Ajax,
and because it was brand new,
he wrote a book describing
all that it could do.

At first the Queen was angry
and she thought that it was crude—
to speak of private duties
seemed unseemly and quite rude.

LEAVE HERE!

ALL ABOUT THE AJAX

JOKES INSTRUCTIONS POEMS

She banished him from court
for having such bad taste
and publicly discussing
what to do with human waste.

AJAX

But Sir John Harrington
was not one to concede.
He felt a flushing toilet
filled a real and basic need.

"What's so wrong," he asked,
with flushing it away?
Would you rather have it stinky
in the palace night and day?"

Stinky Palace

Queen Elizabeth changed her mind
(as queens can sometimes do)
and said she just might try it,
so he built one for her, too.

MAYBE

But the public of the day
did not want something new.
When they ridiculed the toilet
what did clever Sir John do?

DIARRHEA POWER

THAT AJAX TOILET IS A DUMB IDEA!

He said, "Making fun of my toilet
is a really bad idea.
Captain Ajax will be angry,
and he'll give you diarrhea."

OH NO! I GOTTA GO! RIGHT NOW!

CA

CAPTAIN AJAX

1 THEN 2

KING LOUIS (1650s)

King Louis XIV (the fourteenth)
had a special throne
that he sat on at night
when he wasn't alone.

The throne was a toilet
for the king to use
while the lords of his court
told him gossip and news.

For the lords it was an honor,
but the privilege wasn't free.
To get to see the king
they had to pay a fee.

So the fancily dressed lords
spoke to the king of France
while he sat upon his throne
without his royal pants.

FUN FACTS

The king would hold court, write letters, and issue orders while seated on the toilet throne (closestool). This ceremony was called the *petit coucher* (pe-TEE COO-SHAY), which means "little sleep." The lords used this time to ask the king for grants of money or special favors. Not everyone at court used closestools or chamber pots. Nobles often relieved themselves in the corners or stairways of the palace—whichever was closest.

PARIS SEWER TOUR

Did you know
that years ago
in Paris, France,
a city of romance,
people would float
through pipes, on a boat,
under the street
of busy walking feet?

It was a strange, unusual tour
and there's one thing we know for sure—
even dressed in fancy clothes,
guests would want to hold their noses.

But touring was the thing to do,
so wealthy folks took in the view
and "oohed" and "aahed" while floating down
the Paris sewers underground.

ABOVEGROUND

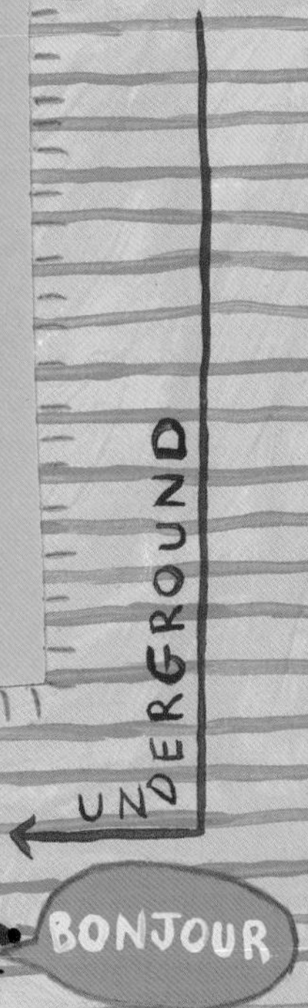

UNDERGROUND

BONJOUR

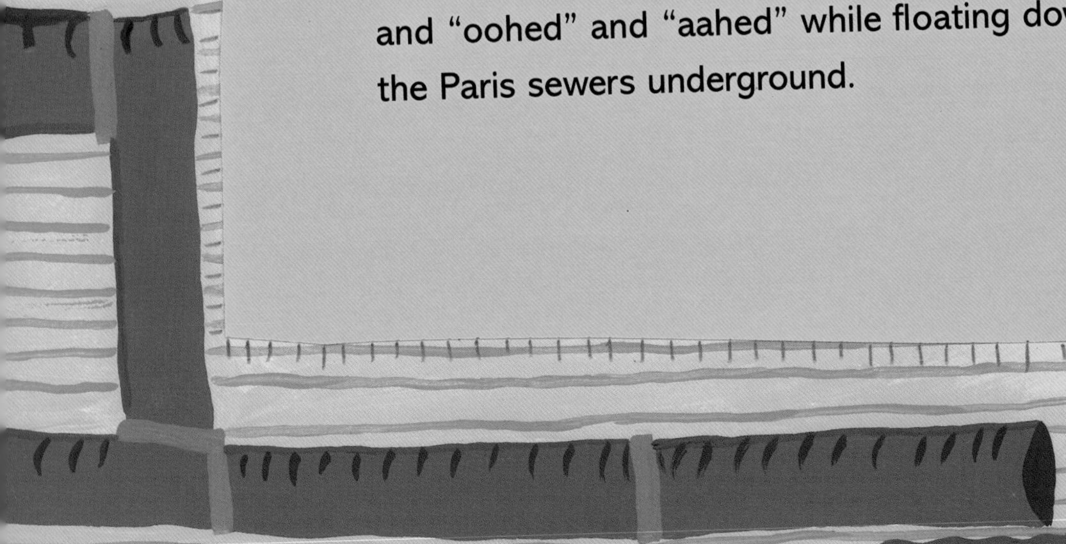

HOLD YOUR NOSE

The Paris sewer tours started in the mid-1800s. The tour boats were outfitted with special wings that cleaned the sides of the pipe as the boat traveled down the tunnel. Lamps on the sides of the pipe lit the way so guests could see where they were going. The water was fast-moving and this helped keep the smell tolerable. The boat tours ended in 1970.

**S
O**

**M
A
N
Y**

**W
A
Y
S**

**T
O**

**F
L
U
S
H**

The toilets of the world
are as different as can be
and range from super basic
to the best in luxury.

Some have you sit,
some have you squat,
if you go a little
or if you go a lot.

If you have to squat
because there is no seat,
there might be handy footrests
to help you place your feet.

Australia's flushing toilets
have options one and two—
for a big or little flush,
depending on what you do.

But if you want fancy,
then the Japanese are king
because they have a toilet
that can do most anything.

It cleans your bottom, blows it dry,
all on a heated seat,
and if you have to sit a while
this toilet can't be beat.

PUSH

PULL

TWO-
BUTTON
PUSH

PUSH
BUTTON

CLOSE
SEAT

PUSH
FOOT
PEDAL

OPEN
STALL DOOR

STAND UP
AFTER
SITTING

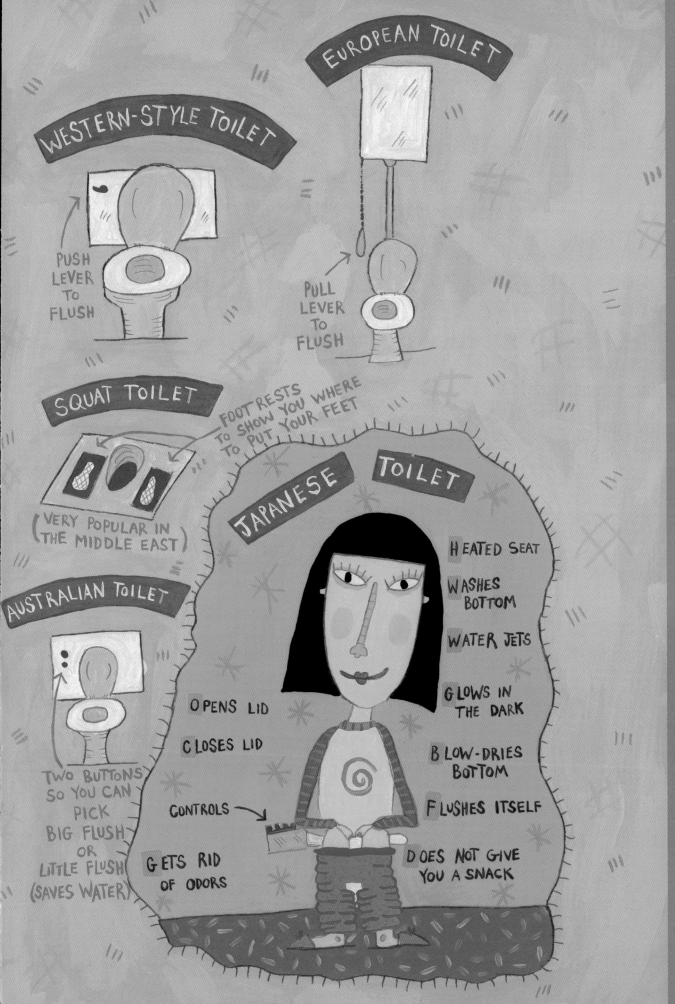

WESTERN-STYLE TOILET

PUSH LEVER TO FLUSH

EUROPEAN TOILET

PULL LEVER TO FLUSH

SQUAT TOILET

FOOT RESTS TO SHOW YOU WHERE TO PUT YOUR FEET

(VERY POPULAR IN THE MIDDLE EAST)

AUSTRALIAN TOILET

TWO BUTTONS SO YOU CAN PICK BIG FLUSH OR LITTLE FLUSH (SAVES WATER)

JAPANESE TOILET

OPENS LID

CLOSES LID

CONTROLS

GETS RID OF ODORS

HEATED SEAT

WASHES BOTTOM

WATER JETS

GLOWS IN THE DARK

BLOW-DRIES BOTTOM

FLUSHES ITSELF

DOES NOT GIVE YOU A SNACK

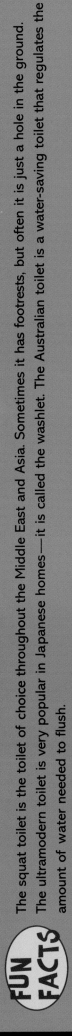

FUN FACTS

The squat toilet is the toilet of choice throughout the Middle East and Asia. Sometimes it has footrests, but often it is just a hole in the ground. The ultramodern toilet is very popular in Japanese homes—it is called the washlet. The Australian toilet is a water-saving toilet that regulates the amount of water needed to flush.

TOILETS IN SPACE

Everything in space
floats all over the place.
Upside down and right-side up,
you can't even drink from a regular cup.

Astronauts are special,
but they're human, too.
They have to use a toilet
the same as we all do.

COME BACK HERE!

With all that floating in the air,
how do toilets work up there?

How do they do it?
How do they stay?
Sitting on the toilet without
floating away?

They strap in their thighs,
they strap in their feet,
and this keeps them attached to the
toilet seat.

But how does flushing pull stuff down,
when gravity's left back on the ground?

Instead of flushing they use air
to suck the waste away from there.

It's not scary, do not fear,
it's just a vacuum for their rears.

GRAVITY

FANS USE AIR
TO SUCK WASTE
AWAY FROM
BOTTOM.

Both male and female astronauts can use the waste collector. Fans create an air current that sucks waste away from the bottom. Each astronaut has a personal urinal funnel, which he or she attaches to a collection hose. Urine is combined with other wastewater and the feces is vacuum-dried and chemically treated to get rid of the smell.

FUN FACTS

FINALLY

We never said it ever.
Not once could it be heard.
We alluded to it plenty,
but then used another word.

So if you want to yell it,
and I know some of you do,
get ready, here it comes.
I'm going to write it just for you.

Let's do it all together.
Not a whisper, give a shout:
"POOPY! POOPY! POOPY!
is what this book's about!"